BROWNIE

THE WAR DOG

VETERANS' BEST FRIEND

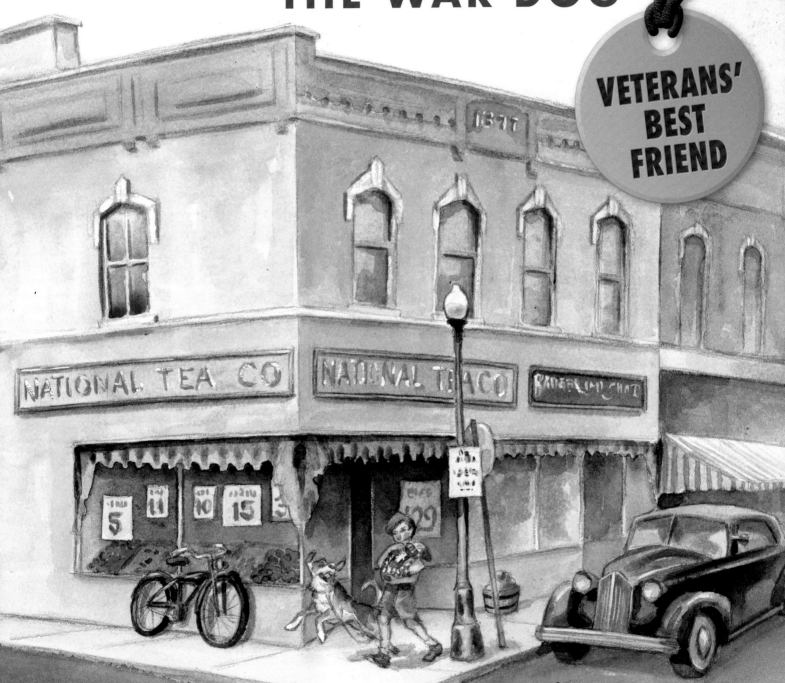

WRITTEN BY KELLY NELSON ILLUSTRATED BY AARON BOYD

2

Spring 1943

Oren dashed out his front door and into the yard next to his. *Oh, no!* His dog, Brownie, was digging up the neighbors' tulips. The cheerful flowers now lay broken at the edge of a deep hole.

Just a year and a half old, Brownie had the energy of a puppy but the body of a full-grown German shepherd mix. The neighbors had already complained to Oren's parents, Freda and Palmer. Such a large dog had no business living in town, they said. Brownie barked too much. He chased cats up trees too much. He pulled clothing off the lines too much. He was simply too much for the small community of King, Wisconsin.

But Oren loved Brownie more than anything. He couldn't imagine giving Brownie up.

As Oren coaxed Brownie back home, his mind raced with ways to say he was sorry to the neighbors. But apologies would have to wait. He was late for school.

Oren and the other students listened to their teacher share the latest news about the Second World War. The war had started in 1939, when Germany invaded other countries. Italy and Japan joined Germany's side, and together they were called the Axis powers. The United States fought on the side of the Allies with Great Britain, the Soviet Union, and other countries. Even though the battles took place far away from Wisconsin, the war was on everyone's mind.

The teacher asked the students how they could help the war effort. At first it seemed like a silly question. They were too young to be soldiers! But soon Oren and his classmates shared what their families were doing to help. Almost everyone had volunteered time, money, or materials to the war effort.

The teacher wrote the ideas on the blackboard. Then she mentioned something that grabbed Oren's attention: the Dogs for Defense program.

After school, Oren couldn't get the Dogs for Defense program out of his head. According to his teacher, some dogs were going to war, like soldiers. They were being trained to follow orders and to do different jobs. The government was asking pet owners to donate their dogs to the program.

Oren's feet led him to the Wisconsin Veterans Home, where his mother worked as a cook. His mom, Freda, was making her famous potato salad. While she worked, Oren told her all about Dogs for Defense.

Soon, the war veterans began to file into the dining hall for dinner. Many of them had fought in the First World War, and Oren had grown up hearing their stories. Some sounded scary. Some were sad. Looking around, he could see that some of the veterans still had injuries from fighting. He thought about their sacrifices. Should he make a big sacrifice, too?

But he couldn't picture his dog helping in a war. Brownie couldn't stay quiet or follow rules. He was a fun pet, but he wouldn't be a good soldier. Would he?

On Saturday morning, Oren biked to the grocery store. Brownie ran alongside him. Oren was on a mission to find a bag of Purina Dog Chow. His teacher had told him the bag would have a Dogs for Defense coupon. If he mailed it in, he would receive an official questionnaire for dog volunteers. He still wasn't sure about this idea, but at least he could find out more.

Soon, the questionnaire arrived in the mail. Oren looked at it with his parents. They both liked the idea of signing Brownie up, which didn't surprise Oren. His family valued military service. His dad, Palmer, had served in the First World War. His older brother Lowell and his sister's husband, Harry, were both fighting in this one.

Oren thought of them now, as he often did. He wondered if they had a dog with their unit. Having a dog around would be comforting. And maybe the dogs were helping to keep soldiers like Lowell and Harry safe.

Oren made his decision. He would send Brownie. Or, at least, he would send the paperwork and see if the army wanted him.

Oren's parents told him to be honest
about how often Brownie barked and
dug holes, so he was. But Oren knew
Brownie was a good dog. With
some help, he could learn to
be an even better dog.

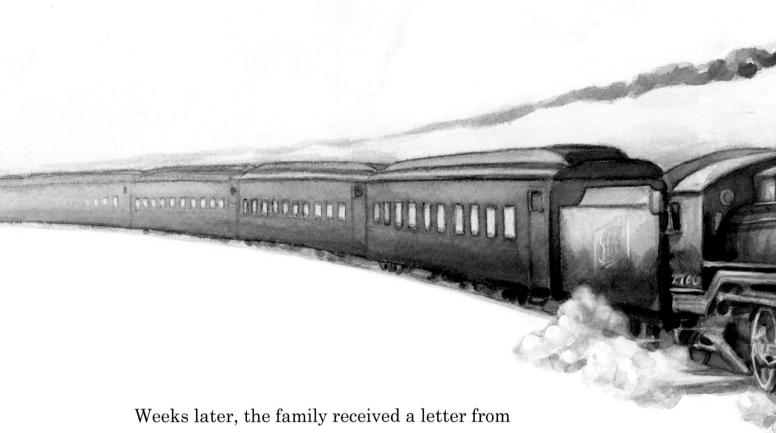

Weeks later, the family received a letter from
Dogs for Defense. The letter instructed them to take
Brownie to the Waupaca Train Depot on May 29, 1943,
for direct shipment to the Fort Robinson Dog Reception &
Training Center in Nebraska. Brownie had been accepted!

At the train station, Oren fought back tears while guiding
Brownie into the wooden shipping crate for his long journey.
Everyone could hear Brownie's howls through the air holes in
the top of the crate. He didn't seem to like being in a box, and
he didn't understand what was happening. Oren tried to be
brave, just like Brownie would have to be brave.

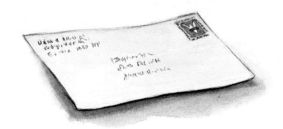

The train's steam engine finally began
to whistle and come to life. It chugged its way
around the bend toward Fort Robinson.

Far away from Oren, Brownie arrived at Fort Robinson.
The US Army veterinarians checked him over. Then, Brownie
met the dog trainers. They decided he would be a sentry. This
meant Brownie would be a lookout, watching for danger. He
would learn how to watch and listen. He would alert his
handler to any strangers he spotted. He would also learn to
protect the soldiers in his unit. One soldier was assigned to be
his handler. He would be the only person to feed, groom, and
handle Brownie once they got to the war.

Brownie's body became very strong thanks to his obstacle
course training. He learned to heel, lie down, sit, and stay.
His handler used hand signals to tell him what to do. Brownie
learned to imitate his handler when he dropped to the ground,
flat as a pancake. When the soldier crawled forward using his
elbows, Brownie learned to crawl forward using his paws.
These moves would help them hide from danger.

Most importantly, Brownie learned not to bark unless his handler gave him a signal. If he barked, the enemy would know right where they were. Brownie learned to be very quiet and to watch his handler for commands at all times. Finally, he was ready.

Brownie and his handler traveled a long way on a ship to an island in the Pacific Ocean. The island was very different from Brownie's home in Wisconsin. There were so many strange smells and sounds. Brownie's nose twitched. He wanted to explore, but he remembered his training. He kept his eyes on his handler and did what he was told.

On the island, the dogs and their handlers had several jobs. They guarded the army's supply tents. They patrolled the beaches looking for signs of enemy soldiers on shore. They patrolled the jungle. If a dog picked up a strange scent or heard an unexpected noise, it would stop in its tracks to alert its handler. The soldiers depended on the dogs to warn them of possible danger. Those warnings could save a soldier's life.

1944

For more than a year, Brownie did his job well. He helped keep the American soldiers in his unit safe. He looked and listened for signs of danger—until one day, danger spotted him first.

September 15, 1944

As Palmer was bringing in the mail, he spotted the Fort Robinson, Nebraska, return address on an envelope. Was it news about Brownie? He rushed to the house to show Freda. Together, they opened the letter from Fort Robinson's quartermaster depot. It said that Brownie had been wounded in the eye. The letter asked whether the family wanted Brownie returned to them. If so, Fort Robinson needed to hear back from them within fifteen days. But the letter warned that Brownie might not be the same friendly family dog they had known before.

Quickly, Freda and Palmer decided two things. One, they wanted Brownie back. And two, they would keep the news of Brownie's return as a surprise for Oren.

When Oren came home from school a few weeks later, his parents stood in front of the house waiting for him. It looked like they had something to tell him. Was it bad news from the war? But they smiled at him, and so he knew it wasn't that.

An old friend was waiting out back to see him, his dad said. Oh, and the friend had four legs. Oren knew what that meant!

Before Oren could take off running, his mom reached for him. She told him that he needed to know a few things first. Brownie had been injured, she explained. He was okay, but he had lost an eye. The army veterinarians had given Brownie a glass eye, but he couldn't see out of it. And he might behave differently than he did before. Oren should move slowly and make sure that Brownie saw him and recognized him.

Oren promised to be careful. Nervously, he rounded the back corner of the house.

There was Brownie, lying calmly under a tree. The dog lifted his head as soon as he heard Oren coming. When Brownie saw Oren, he sat up to get a better look at his long-lost friend, but he didn't bark. Quivering with excitement, he whined and whimpered, but he didn't race over to jump on Oren.

Oren remembered to move slowly. He spoke gently. He told Brownie that it was okay and that he was home now. But it wasn't until Oren gestured with his hands that Brownie came to him. A moment later, Oren was laughing and crying, covered in joyful dog kisses.

As Brownie rested and readjusted to life at home, his family watched him closely. They followed the army's instructions to keep the house quiet for the first few weeks.

The army had given them other instructions as well. No one should ever tease Brownie, sneak up on him, or surprise him. They should never give Brownie the command "sic 'em" or say anything else that would sound like an order to attack.

Slowly, they reintroduced him to people outside the family. When Oren's friends came over, his parents watched Brownie carefully. Would he attack someone if he didn't know them? But Brownie was friendly to everyone he met. The trainers at Fort Robinson had done a good job preparing Brownie for family life after his time serving overseas.

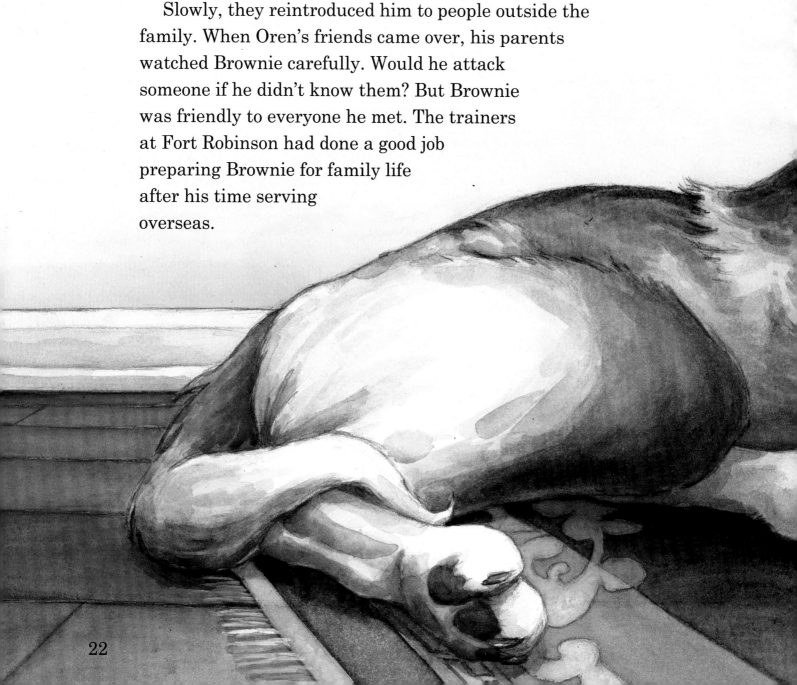

Once Brownie had a chance to rest and heal, he began to follow Oren everywhere. Oren spent as much time with Brownie as he could. His favorite thing to do was fish for walleye off the shores of Rainbow Lake with Brownie's warm body leaning against his. He had his old friend back.

The biggest difference that Oren noticed was how quiet Brownie had become! He used to bark at anything that moved, but not anymore. Now, he silently watched as folks in town went about their day. Instead of complaining, the neighbors now praised Brownie's brave service and good manners.

Brownie's glass eye looked so real, many people never noticed it. But the family did have to be careful because of his limited eyesight. Brownie couldn't see cars or people coming from the left. Since their home was near a highway, Oren kept Brownie either close to him or tied up to keep him away from the road.

Life returned to normal. Oren went to school, and Palmer and Freda went to work. But Brownie was no longer happy to stay home and do nothing. When he had been overseas, he had an important job to do every day.

Brownie began to meet Freda at the door when she left for work in the morning. Soon, he started going with her. Freda would smile as Brownie fell into step with her all the way to the Wisconsin Veterans Home.

Every day, Brownie walked Freda to the dining hall. Then he headed to the rows of cottages by the lake to visit veterans and their spouses. Many of the people who lived at the veterans home had grown up on family farms. They enjoyed activities that reminded them of their younger years. They grew big vegetable gardens and delighted in the daily visits from the big, lovable dog.

Each day, Brownie visited the folks who lived at the veterans home. Brownie always seemed to know who needed company the most. He even stopped in to see the man in charge, Commandant Colonel Carl Brosius.

After a full day of treats and pats, a tired Brownie would meet Freda back at the dining hall for their walk home.

The family laughed when they noticed that Brownie rarely ate meals at home anymore. He was too full from all the treats the veterans fed him!

Oren was proud to know that Brownie had bravely served his fellow soldiers during the war and was now serving his fellow veterans at home.

About a year after Brownie returned home, the Second World War came to an end. The US and its allies had won. Everyone in the town of King celebrated, including the veterans at the Wisconsin Veterans Home. Brownie celebrated with them.

For many years, Brownie joined his fellow veterans in the Memorial Day and Fourth of July parades. With his head held high, he marched as a proud soldier and a veteran's best friend.

Author's Note

The year 2019 proved to be a very challenging one for my family. My dad, a Korean War veteran, had begun to need more care than our family could provide for him. We toured the Wisconsin Veterans Home at King in hopes that he could be cared for there. While touring the facility, we viewed the Wisconsin Veterans Home Museum. At the museum, I saw a display that included black and white photographs of a dog named Brownie and the brief story of his young owner, Oren Kendley, who donated him for service in the Second World War.

As a passionate dog lover, I wanted to learn more about Brownie and Oren's story. I learned that Oren had passed away many years ago, so I began to research Oren's living family members. I eventually made contact with Joan Yohr, Oren's niece. Joan had written a history of her family called *When Lilacs Bloom*, which included a chapter about her Uncle Oren's war dog named Brownie. Joan was just a little girl when Brownie was a puppy, and she had fond memories of her uncle's dog. The history Joan wrote provided much of the information I needed to write this book.

Brownie and Oren (right) with a friend in 1945.
Photo courtesy of the Wisconsin Veterans Home at King

In addition to recording family memories, Joan collected valuable artifacts, including photographs of Brownie and Oren, a copy of the letter sent from the quartermaster depot to the Kendley family before Brownie's return, and Brownie's honorable discharge certificate. Throughout the years, Joan made sure that all of Brownie's photographs and wartime paperwork stayed with the family. She eventually donated all those items to the Wisconsin Veterans Museum in Madison, Wisconsin, where they can be viewed today.

Joan is now a dear friend of mine, having provided help and encouragement as I worked to transform Brownie and Oren's story into the book you're reading now.

I truly believe that both Oren and Brownie are heroes who deserve to be honored and remembered. From the beginning, my sincerest aim has been to tell this remarkable animal's story in a truthful and heartfelt way. I hope that by reading his story, many others may come to understand and appreciate all that Brownie did for his family, his country, and his fellow veterans.

This book is dedicated to my loving parents, Tom and Sandy Rhode.
–Kelly

To (my pup) Gretel, for all the miles shared. Be well.
–Aaron

Published by the Wisconsin Historical Society Press
Publishers since 1855

The Wisconsin Historical Society helps people connect to the
past by collecting, preserving, and sharing stories. Founded in
1846, the Society is one of the nation's finest historical institutions.
Join the Wisconsin Historical Society: wisconsinhistory.org/membership

Publication of this book was made possible in part by a gift from Larry Sawyer
and Debra McDowall.

Printed in Canada
Designed by Wisconsin Historical Society Press

28 27 26 25 24   1 2 3 4 5

Library of Congress Cataloging-in-Publication Data
Names: Nelson, Kelly, 1972–   author. | Boyd, Aaron, illustrator.
Title: Brownie the war dog : veterans' best friend / story by Kelly Nelson ;
    drawings by Aaron Boyd.
Description: Madison : Wisconsin Historical Society Press, [2024] |
    Audience: Ages 8–11 | Audience: Grades 4–6
Identifiers: LCCN 2023053688 (print) | LCCN 2023053689 (e-book) | ISBN
    9781976600135 (hardcover) | ISBN 9781976600142 (epub)
Subjects: LCSH: Brownie (Dog), 1941–1949—Juvenile literature. | Dogs—War
    Use—United States—Juvenile literature. | Kendley, Oren—Juvenile
    literature. | World War, 1939–1945—Wisconsin—Biography—Juvenile
    literature. | United States. Army. K-9 Corps—Biography—Juvenile
    literature. | Veterans—Wisconsin—Biography—Juvenile literature.
Classification: LCC D810.A65 B766 2024 (print) | LCC D810.A65 (e-book) |
    DDC 355.4/24—dc23/eng/20240220
LC record available at https://lccn.loc.gov/2023053688
LC e-book record available at https://lccn.loc.gov/2023053689

♾ The paper used in this publication meets the minimum requirements of the
American National Standard for Information Sciences—Permanence of Paper
for Printed Library Materials, ANSI Z39.48-1992.